# CAPITALISM, LABOUR AND POLITICS IN RURAL INDIA

# CAPITALISM, LABOUR AND POLITICS IN RURAL INDIA

Pratyush Chandra

*Published for*
**Odisha Shramjivi Union**

CAPITALISM, LABOUR AND POLITICS IN RURAL INDIA
Pratyush Chandra



First Published 2010

ISBN 978-93-5002-101-9



*Published by*
**AAKAR BOOKS**
28 E Pocket IV, Mayur Vihar Phase I, Delhi 110 091
Phone : 011 2279 5505 Telefax : 011 2279 5641
aakarbooks@gmail.com; www.aakarbooks.com

*Supported by*
**SRUTI**
Q 1, Hauz Khas Enclave, New Delhi 110 016
Web : www.sruti.org.in
E-mail : sruti@vsnl.com

*Printed at*
Mudrak, Delhi 110 091

# Contents

# Preface

In recent years, rural Orissa has been the hub of rural struggles. While many of these struggles are explicitly linked with the displacement drive initiated by neoliberal competition for attracting corporate capital investment in which the political elite of various regions, including Orissa, has been engaged, their trajectory too – the forms and contents of rural mobilisations and organisations – is defined by the internal, but open-ended, political economic configuration of rural Orissa. We must try to develop an understanding of this configuration that can help in formulating a framework for comprehending the nature of these rural struggles. We cannot take these struggles at their face value, satisfying ourselves with the vocalisation of internal perceptions – of their leadership or any segment within; rather we must locate them in the larger political economy and its contradictions. It is not that these perceptions, motivations and ideologies do not matter, but they have to be understood in terms of the composition of these struggles and the context. In fact, we start with a brief critique of these perceptions, which will help us introduce our theme and initiate our discussion.

Here we have extensively relied on the NSSO (National Sample Survey Organisation) data to obtain an overview of rural differentiation in India in general and Orissa in particular. However, the focus is clearly to comprehend the conceptual and political implications of the evolving rural scenario in India.

# 1

# Capitalist Transformation in Rural Areas – What Does it Signify?

Generally, when we talk about capitalist development in a society, our focus is on industrial progress – on the growth of industries. Commercialisation and monetisation of the economy are definitely taken into account, but they are considered to be, and rightly so, tools of the expansion of capitalism, not the capitalist system itself. So for many, the recent reckless drive to sell off resources in Orissa to corporate capital seems to be heralding capitalism. It is forgotten that such formidable will to industrialise is dependent at least to some extent on the political economic interests organically grounded in the Oriya economy, which are now attracting global capital market.

Even when agriculture is discussed, measurements of capitalist penetration are essentially the extent of mechanisation, capitalisation and proletarianisation (number of landless wage workers, i.e., in absolute terms). A strong presence of petty tenant farmers, simple commodity producers, the exploitation of the unwaged (bonded or family) labour, extra-"economic" means of exploitation (labour extraction) and oppression are all considered, by a large section of experts, to be symptoms of *lack* of capitalism in Indian agriculture. These "non-capitalist" modes and relations of production demonstrate the inability of Indian capitalism in transforming the rural economy – testifying its "semi-feudal", "comprador", compromising attitude towards the non-capitalist political economic rural elite etc. On the other hand, there are many scholars and activists who foreground the articulation of "the other" in this *lack* – the resistance of Indian peasantry and subaltern to the processes of primitive accumulation and capitalist penetration. In regions like Orissa where we find a strong presence of tribal communities, this resistance is conceived not as derived from locally grounded contradictions in which these communities are themselves enmeshed, but as resilience derived from the incompatibility of their cultural economy with the "external" forces of capitalism.

The political-organisational leadership of rural struggles have largely been informed by these two approaches. So they have implied drastically different political economic programmes and intellectual outputs. However, there are subtle similarities too. Firstly, they adhere to a purist and a stagist conception of capitalism. Their concept of the non-capitalist nature of the rural economy (even if they themselves sometimes call it petty bourgeois) and its political economic persistence (in their view, resistance) poses a notion of "pure" capitalism. As an abstraction, the idea of non-capitalism can definitely help in modelling the internality of local structures; however to pose it as an autonomous concrete having an external-internal relationship with capitalism brings in the notion of pure capitalism from the backdoor. How even seemingly non-capitalist structures come to embody capitalist relations (which include their contradictory nature) is not a question that becomes their object of study. For them the persistence of non-capitalist structures is the effect of their ability to resist.

Secondly, both approaches put agriculture on the receiving end of capitalist development, and stress on the rural-urban divide; however, they obviously differ as regard to the moral of the capitalist teleology. A concomitant product of this stress is the perception of rural homogeneity. At this level, theoreticians and practitioners of the first approach will object, because they profess to question and fight semi-feudalism, thus recognising the reality of rural stratification. But since the "stage" of their struggle is purportedly anti-feudal, anti-comprador, anti-bureaucratic, for all practical purposes their analyses are lost in the task of identifying feudal elements and comprador agents, thus constructing a homogenised revolutionary other – the *narod* (people).

Let us confront these approaches a bit more in order to approach our primary task of understanding capitalism in Indian agriculture.

It is a truism that rural and urban are unequal spheres, both compositionally and relationally. They have different internalities (formed around two very different kinds of production spheres – agriculture and industry), which make their exchange unequal. Relationships between different sectors within an economy can never be equal, since they are competitive. So the "divide" is definitely present – it is this divide which is termed as inter-sectoral competition in capitalism. Through competition, value is transferred from one sector to another, from one industry to another. This transfer is inevitable under commodity relations, but it cannot be called exploitative, unless the subordination of a sector entails an unmediated mobilisation of unpaid surplus labour (value) from direct producers (unwaged or waged). Hence exploitation has to be located intra-sectorally. The rural-urban divide and the transfer of value from agriculture to industry that it entails cannot be understood in terms of exploitation, as defined above. The divide and the transfer are competitive and competition redistributes value (and therefore, profit) across society.

One can object to this perception by posing the example of usury and mercantile capital, which have been the bulwarks of capitalist penetration in agriculture and rural economy. But their penetration becomes exploitation only when they are internalised by the agrarian structure. If they are financiers of the agrarian capitalists who are the main organisers of production, their relationship with the latter is redistributive. At the most it can be extractive, but not exploitative. However as part of "social" capital their relationship with labour, even if the latter directly works for an agrarian capitalist, is definitely exploitative. But the financiers' relationship with petty or simple commodity producers who engage in family labour is a bit subtle. It can be both extractive and exploitative, depending on the former's ability to influence or control the production process.

Understanding the internality or internal structure of the rural economy and the mode of its (re)production becomes very important in order to comprehend the terrain from which a rural struggle emerges, and which defines its character. In a class-divided rural society, posing the rural-urban divide as victimisation and talking about rural homogeneity is ideological, using the exploited ones, the labourers, as cannon-fodder in the competitive and concession fight of the rural elite. It is at this level that perceptions, motivations and ideologies find meaning.

As mentioned earlier the persistence of non/pre-capitalist "modes" of production in India has long mesmerised the progressive intellectuals and activists, a vast majority of whom consider its existence as a reminder of the amphibian (semi-feudal, semi-capitalist) nature of India's political economy and its underdevelopment – overloaded with pre-capitalist "vestiges," while others call them subsistence economies, challenging mainstream capitalism. We believe that the notion of "separate" non-capitalist modes of production is problematic if it is not predicated upon an understanding of a capitalist socio-economic formation that accommodates these modes as relative forms of accumulation and exploitation feeding the social reproduction of capitalism. This paper while discussing the specificities of rural economy will also demonstrate how vestigial forms acquire new meanings within larger political economic processes of capital accumulation and social reproduction. Only this will allow us to interpret rural struggles and recognise their potential strength in protecting the interests of labour against capital.

**Passive Revolution and Agrarian Transformation**

Unevenness is intrinsic to capitalist development. The unevenness of geographical developments in general reflects

> ...the different ways in which different social groups have materially embedded their modes of sociality into the web of life, understood as an evolving socio-ecological system... Capitalist activity is always grounded somewhere. Diverse material processes (physical, ecological as well as social) must be appropriated, used, bent and re-shaped to the purposes and paths of capital accumulation.[1]

In the grounding of capitalist activity this diversity materialises into geographical unevenness. David Harvey writes further in his *Limits to Capital*:

> The upshot is that the development of the space economy of capitalism is beset by counterposed and contradictory tendencies. On the one hand spatial barriers and regional distinctions must be broken down. Yet the means to achieve that entail the production of new geographical differentiations which form new spatial barriers to be overcome. The geographical organization of capitalism internalizes the contradictions within the value form. This is what is meant by the concept of the inevitable uneven development of capitalism.[2]

The subcontinental nature of the Indian economy is bound to house various "geographical differentiations." The unevenness of capitalist development in India is at least partly due to the diverse forms that the institutionalisation of economic relations took during colonial times. The plethora of land tenurial arrangements that the British effected in rural areas led to "the regionalization of class and factional struggle," which essentially implied territorially based alliances and conflicts between various factions of capital, the local state, and social classes. During the struggle for

Independence and after its attainment we find this regionalisation shaping the contours of political economic institutions. The highly differentiated social infrastructures that independent India inherited were largely kept as they were.

Orissa, which was constructed out of many princely states along with areas under the direct control of the British, is an uneven terrain of social relations. There were diverse forms of production relations that had to articulate with one another.

After independence, the political setup in India was constructed by accommodating various regional class configurations, without directly challenging the local hegemonies. The unitary tendency emanated from their articulation within the national economic development by market integration through an intensified monetisation and commercialisation of the local economies. This process was aided by the straitjacketing of regional hegemonies in the discursive milieu of anti-colonial nationalism and democratic political competition. Rajni Kothari has correctly pointed out:

> "The role of the centre and in particular of the Indian National Congress in mediating the various coalitional strains in the states has been profound in weaving together the heterogeneity of Indian society into a common national political framework. At the same time, the consolidation of state power in the framework of an increasing formalization of the federal constitution has made for typical patterns of institutional diffusion and decentralization. The result is a "mix" of centre peripheral relationships."[3]

Indian federalism was the result of the "coalition-making" at the time when India got its Independence. Autonomy in regional politics and mobilisation provided space and time to the regional class interests and hegemonies to adjust with the larger political economic processes in the country. The Indian state, as the embodiment of the generalised interests of the hegemonic forces in the country, relied on a gradual trickle-down, along with transitive Midas' effects of socio-economic changes, to *integrate* the local and peripheral hegemonies.

Apparently, after Independence and especially from the 1970s, the Indian polity witnessed a tremendous upsurge in casteist and identitarian competition, which in our view, was not really a crisis; rather it represented the success of the Indian political economy in transforming the traditional caste hierarchy into a ground for waging a competitive struggle for the accumulation of economic and political power. This competition is representative of the inclusive nature of development in India – however, as competition is unequal, so is the inclusion. Underneath the surface structure of caste and identitarian conflicts (a competition for representation), there lay a deep structure of intra/inter-class conflicts that marked political economic transformation in the country.

Though the anti-zamindari laws against rentier landlordism (which was concentrated among the upper castes) were formulated, they were not implemented systematically. But the agencies of the market did breed the classes of rural bourgeoisie and petty bourgeoisie, who specialised in market-oriented production or distribution. They challenged the hegemony of upper caste landlords – including their control over state bureaucracy and politics.

On the other hand, there emerged an underclass majority under the effect of market-induced pauperisation and proletarianisation. Various sections of this class too have frequently associated themselves on identitarian and caste lines; however, it will need a vast historical analysis to assess the impact of class struggle on caste conflicts and vice versa, a task which we cannot undertake here. In the following section we discuss some statistics that help us in understanding class formation, especially the character of the 'underclass', in rural India.

# 2

# Rural Differentiation– A Statistical Survey

Even before independence, nationalist leaders like Acharya Narendra Deva who were involved in the creation of a homogeneous peasant organisation to pose a united front against the British domination in rural India were aware that, "the peasantry is not a homogeneous class. It has many class divisions". Furthermore, "the number of landless peasants is ever on the increase and if today these internal conflicts have not come to the surface, in the coming days they are bound to accentuate. Class divisions within the peasantry will slowly mature..."[4]

Swami Sahajanand Saraswati who was one of the main proponents and organisers of a united Kisan movement in the country, was more blunt in regard to the problems of imposing homogeneity, when he noted in 1944:

> They (middle and big cultivators) are using the Kisan Sabha for their benefit and gain, while we are using or rather trying to use them to strengthen the Sabha, till the lowest strata of the peasantry are awakened to their real economic and political interests and needs and have become class conscious... It is they, the semi-proletariat or the agricultural labourers who have very little land or no land at all, and the petty cultivators, who anyhow squeeze a most meagre living out of the land they cultivate and eke out their existence, who are the kisans of our

> thinking...and who make and must constitute the Kisan Sabha ultimately.[5]

Post-independence India shows three typical effects of development on the rural population – a gradual fragmentation of landholdings, increasing landlessness and the creation of footloose labour. Let us discuss the statistics regarding these phenomena, but keeping in mind the warning that Kautsky and Lenin voiced a century ago:

> ...if agricultural statistics are taken in general, and uncritically, it is quite easy to discover in the capitalist mode of production a tendency to transform modern nations into hunting tribes.[6]

## 1. Land Marginalisation

Throughout the so-called third world countries (which includes India), rural areas still accommodate the majority of their population. The obvious conclusion is that in these areas agriculture continues to be the major source of employment, income and livelihood. Furthermore, in this situation of rural overpopulation, land marginalisation and the consequent domination of small farms is bound to happen. Thus, the average farm size in Africa and Asia in the 1990s was 1.6 hectares. It is assumed that the increasing subdivision of land holdings indicates the absorption of the rising population into agriculture. Though apparently true, it also suggests that an ever-increasing portion of the agrarian population has to supplement their farm income by engaging in waged or other non-farm activities.

### *Operational Holdings*

In India too, the average size of operational landholdings has been declining unabatedly, which, according to the National Sample Survey's estimation, stood at 1.06 hectares in 2002-03 (however, the census figure in this regard, was 1.32 hectares in 2000-01). As evident from Table 1, the average size has fallen by around 60% from 1960-61. However, the rate of growth in the number of operational holdings has

**Table 1: Distribution of Operational Holdings in India (in %)**

| *Category* | *1960-61* | | *1970-71* | | *1981-82* | | *1991-92* | | *2002-03* | | | |
|---|---|---|---|---|---|---|---|---|---|---|---|---|
| | | | | | | | | | *Kharif* | | *Rabi* | |
| | *No.* | *Area* | *No.* | *Area* | *No.* | *Area* | *No.* | *Area* | *No.* | *Area* | *No.* | *Area* |
| Marginal | 39.1 | 6.9 | 45.8 | 9.2 | 56.0 | 11.5 | 62.8 | 15.6 | 69.7 | 22.6 | 70.0 | 21.7 |
| Small | 22.6 | 12.3 | 22.4 | 14.8 | 19.3 | 16.6 | 17.8 | 18.7 | 16.3 | 20.9 | 15.9 | 20.3 |
| Semi-medium | 19.8 | 20.7 | 17.7 | 22.6 | 14.2 | 23.6 | 12.0 | 24.1 | 9.0 | 22.5 | 8.9 | 22.3 |
| Medium | 14.0 | 31.2 | 11.1 | 30.5 | 8.6 | 30.1 | 6.1 | 26.4 | 4.2 | 22.2 | 4.4 | 23.1 |
| Large | 4.5 | 29.0 | 3.1 | 23.0 | 1.9 | 18.2 | 1.3 | 15.2 | 0.8 | 11.8 | 0.8 | 12.5 |
| All Sizes | 100 | 100 | 100 | 100 | 100 | 100 | 100 | 100 | 100 | 100 | 100 | 100 |
| Average farm size | 2.63 | | 2.20 | | 1.67 | | 1.34 | | | | 1.06 | |

Marginal - <1 ha, Small – 1.01-2.00 ha, Semi-Medium – 2.01-4.00, Medium – 4.01-10.00, Large – 10.00+ *Source: NSS Report 492* significantly slowed down in the recent years (it was 24.5% in 1981-82, 31.5% in 1991-92 and 8.4% in 2002-03). Table 1 demonstrates that over the years the peasantry has been pauperised, with 63% of the operational holdings being of less than 1 hectare, and around 82% below 2 hectares. According to the Census, in 2000-01, the average farm size for the marginal category was 0.40, for the small category it was 1.41, for the semi-medium category 2.72, for the medium category 5.8 and for large farmers it was 17.18.[7]

**Table 2: Percentage distribution of household operational holdings**

| *Category* | *1960-61* | *1971-72* | *1981-82* | *1991-92* | *2002-03* |
|---|---|---|---|---|---|
| Nil | 26.9 | 27.4 | 26.1 | 21.8 | 31.9 |
| Marginal | 30.7 | 32.9 | 41.1 | 48.3 | 47.1 |
| Small | 16.2 | 16.4 | 14.5 | 14.2 | 11.2 |
| Semi-Medium | 13.8 | 12.9 | 10.6 | 9.7 | 6.2 |
| Medium | 9.4 | 8.1 | 6.3 | 4.9 | 2.9 |
| Large | 3.0 | 2.2 | 1.4 | 1.1 | 0.5 |
| All Sizes | 100 | 100 | 100 | 100 | 100 |

Nil – 0-0.002, Marginal – 0.002-1 ha, Small – 1.01-2.00 ha, Semi-Medium – 2.01-4.00, Medium – 4.01-10.00, Large – 10.00+

*Source: NSS Report 493*

However, in order to present a better picture of the rural scenario, one must include those rural households which do not operate any land in the distribution. In fact, such inclusion of the operationally landless drastically alters the picture of rural society as presented in Table 1. Table 2 shows that the only class of households that witnessed an increase in percentage distribution during 1991-2003 was the "nil" category, i.e. that the category containing those households which have zero operational land. The data records a drastic increase in the rate of growth of landlessness, which affects severely the percentage share of other categories in the distribution of household. While from 1971 onwards there had been a progressive decrease in the percentage share of the "nil" category, from 1991 onwards we find a 10% increase.

Even if we accept the apologia of the NSSO that the 2002-03 data might have been affected by the fact that it was collected only during the *kharif* season, the enormous size of the "nil" category cannot be accounted for fully by any correction (though it could have presented a better picture of the marginal category, which too declined like other higher categories in the following table). On the whole, 79% of rural households throughout India either does not operate any land or are of marginal farmers; the figure exceeds 90% if we include small farmers.

If we take absolute alienation from land as a measure of proletarianisation, it is now established that there is a continuous increase of rural landlessness in the country. In 1987-88 the proportion of the rural landless (who did not have any access to land) among the total number of rural households in India was 35.4%, which increased to 38.7% in 1993-94. In 1999-2000 the figure was 40.9.[8] The following data (Table 3) further corroborates the intensity of proletarianisation among total number of agricultural labour households (which includes the class of poor peasantry – i.e. those who have some land but have to rely on wage labour or "self-employment" for their subsistence):

**Table 3: Agricultural labour Households with/without access to any cultivable land**

| | *1983* | *1987-88* | *1993-94* | *1999-00* | *2004-05* |
|---|---|---|---|---|---|
| Households without cultivable land | 55.9 | 52.2 | 57 | 57.3 | 62.1 |
| Households with some land | 44.1 | 47.8 | 43 | 42.7 | 37.9 |

*Source*: RLE, Report on General Characteristics of Rural Labour Households, 1999-00 and NSS 61" round

Let us now try to understand the scenario in Orissa. Table 5 shows a very high increase in the share of marginal farmers in the distribution of operational holdings in Orissa. If we reconstruct the data by including the landless and subdividing the category of marginal farmers, the picture is slightly different from the all India level. In Orissa, there was a marginal increase in the number of the landless, but the number of the poorest among marginal farmers saw a formidable growth (!). In Table 4 marginal farmers have been divided in two classes – the size class of 0.002-0.5 and of 0.5-1.0 ha. It is the first size-class that bulged the most from 1991-92 to 2002-03.

**Table 4: Percentage of households in each size class of household operational holding (Orissa)**

| *Size class of household operational holding (ha)* | *Percentage of Households* 1991-92 | 2002-03 |
|---|---|---|
| Nil | 27.2 | 27.54 |
| 0.002-0.5 | 27.35 | 38.92 |
| 0.5-1.0 | 16.10 | 17.58 |
| 1.0-2.0 | 17.87 | 11.28 |
| 2.0-3.0 | 6.73 | 2.94 |
| 3.0-4.0 | 2.04 | 0.88 |
| 4.0-5.0 | 1.31 | 0.34 |
| 5.0-10.0 | 1.17 | 0.48 |
| 10.0-20.0 | 0.22 | 0.04 |
| >20.0 | - | - |

*Source:* Calculated on the basis of NSS Reports 408 & 493

**Table 5: Changes in percentage distribution of operational holdings and area operated in Orissa**

| *Category* | *1970-71* | | *1981-82* | | *1991-92* | | *2002-03* | |
|---|---|---|---|---|---|---|---|---|
| | *No. of holdings* | *Area* | *No. of holdings* | *Area* | *No. of holdings* | *Area* | *No. of holdings* | *Area* |
| Marginal | 54.5 | 18.6 | 54.5 | 17.0 | 60.0 | 22.1 | 78.4 | 43.0 |
| Small | 25.8 | 27.3 | 26.1 | 26.5 | 24.3 | 30.2 | 15.2 | 28.7 |
| Semi-medium | 13.9 | 27.1 | 14.1 | 26.2 | 12.0 | 27.9 | 5.2 | 18.8 |
| Medium | 5.3 | 21.6 | 4.6 | 17.8 | 3.4 | 16.2 | 1.1 | 8.6 |
| Large | 0.6 | 5.5 | 0.7 | 12.5 | 0.3 | 3.7 | 0.1 | 0.9 |

*Source:* NSS Report 492

A cursory comparison of Table 1 and Table 5 shows that quite unlike the all India level, the concentration of operational holding is quite low in Orissa. In Table 6 we give a comparison of Gini's coefficient of concentration at the national and Orissa levels. This is a comment on the state and function of the rural society in Orissa - the predominance of landholdings of unviable sizes.

**Table 6: Trend in Gini's Coefficient of Concentration of Operational Holdings**

| *Years* | *India* | *Orissa* |
|---|---|---|
| 1970-71 | 0.586 | 0.466 |
| 1981-82 | 0.629 | 0.504 |
| 1991-91 | 0.641 | 0.462 |
| 2002-03 | 0.624 | 0.381 |

*Source*: NSS Report 492

### *Ownership Holdings*

Let us now examine the land ownership data. At the all India level 10% of the rural households were landless (in terms of ownership). The average area owned per rural household is 0.725 hectare. If we exclude the landless households, then the average area owned is 0.806. On the other hand, in Orissa, landlessness is 9.56%, while the average area owned per rural household is considerably low in comparison to the national average. Including the landless, it is 0.483 ha, and excluding them, it amounts to 0.534 ha.

Table 7 shows the overall skewed nature of the size distribution of ownership holdings at the all India level. Around 50 % of the total households own just 2% of the total area, around 60% own less than 6 percent, and around 80% of the total households own only 23% of the total area. Further, around 9.5% of the rural households own 56% of the total land. This demonstrates a formidable concentration of ownership holdings, measured by Gini's coefficient.

**Table 7: Cumulative Percentage Distribution of Households and Area Owned Over Size-classes of Household-ownership Holding in Different NSS Rounds**

| *Category* | *1960-61* | | *1970-71* | | *1981-82* | | *1991-92* | | *2002-03* | |
|---|---|---|---|---|---|---|---|---|---|---|
| | *No.* | *Area* | *No.* | *Area* | *No.* | *Area* | *No.* | *Area* | *No.* | *Area* |
| <0.002 | 11.68 | 0.00 | 9.64 | 0.00 | 11.33 | 0.00 | 11.25 | 0.00 | 10.04 | 0.01 |
| <0.21 | 37.90 | 0.54 | 37.42 | 0.69 | 39.93 | 0.90 | 42.40 | 1.31 | 50.60 | 2.08 |
| <0.41 | 44.21 | 1.59 | 44.87 | 2.07 | 48.21 | 2.75 | 51.36 | 3.80 | 60.15 | 5.83 |
| <1.01 | 66.06 | 7.59 | 62.62 | 9.76 | 66.61 | 12.22 | 71.88 | 16.93 | 79.67 | 23.02 |
| <2.01 | 75.22 | 19.98 | 78.11 | 24.44 | 81.34 | 28.71 | 85.30 | 35.52 | 90.48 | 43.40 |
| <3.01 | 83.51 | 31.55 | 86.00 | 37.14 | 88.61 | 42.55 | 91.86 | 50.90 | 94.76 | 57.21 |
| <4.01 | 88.08 | 40.52 | 90.00 | 46.36 | 92.12 | 52.09 | 94.58 | 60.10 | 96.51 | 65.37 |
| <6.01 | 93.17 | 54.49 | 94.67 | 60.93 | 96.02 | 66.73 | 97.39 | 73.33 | 98.38 | 77.46 |
| <8.01 | 95.64 | 64.15 | 96.71 | 70.19 | 97.66 | 75.55 | 98.50 | 80.74 | 99.14 | 84.44 |
| <10.01 | 97.15 | 71.75 | 97.88 | 77.09 | 98.57 | 81.99 | 99.12 | 86.17 | 99.47 | 88.45 |
| <12.01 | 98.01 | 77.08 | 98.55 | 81.89 | 99.00 | 85.73 | 99.40 | 89.18 | 99.63 | 90.83 |
| <20.01 | 99.40 | 88.87 | 99.59 | 92.14 | 99.76 | 94.57 | 99.85 | 95.69 | 99.90 | 97.02 |
| Gini's coeff. of concent. | 0.73 | | 0.71 | | 0.71 | | 0.71 | | 0.74 | |

*Source*: NSS Report 491

**Table 8: Percentage Distribution of Households and area Owned Over Five Broad Classes (2002-2003)**

| *All India* | *Year* | *Percentage of households* | | | | | *Percentage of area owned* | | | | |
|---|---|---|---|---|---|---|---|---|---|---|---|
| | | *Mar* | *Sm* | *SMed* | *Med* | *Large* | *Mar* | *Sm* | *SMed* | *Med* | *Large* |
| | 2003 | 79.60 | 10.80 | 6.00 | 3.00 | 0.60 | 23.05 | 20.38 | 21.98 | 23.08 | 11.55 |
| | 1992 | 71.88 | 13.42 | 9.28 | 4.54 | 0.88 | 16.93 | 18.59 | 24.58 | 26.07 | 13.83 |
| | 1982 | 66.64 | 14.70 | 10.78 | 6.45 | 1.42 | 12.22 | 16.49 | 23.58 | 29.83 | 18.07 |
| | 1972 | 62.62 | 15.49 | 11.94 | 7.83 | 2.12 | 9.76 | 14.68 | 21.92 | 30.73 | 22.91 |
| Orissa | 2003 | 85.50 | 9.70 | 3.70 | 0.90 | 0.10 | 41.52 | 27.06 | 19.72 | 9.98 | 1.78 |
| | 1992 | 75.15 | 14.42 | 7.34 | 2.40 | 0.12 | 26.37 | 27.16 | 25.99 | 18.08 | 2.40 |
| | 1982 | 66.06 | 20.84 | 9.31 | 3.42 | 0.37 | 19.88 | 29.73 | 25.04 | 19.50 | 5.84 |
| | 1971 | 68.94 | 18.08 | 9.04 | 3.52 | 0.42 | 20.45 | 26.95 | 25.88 | 20.72 | 6.00 |

Source: NSS Report 491

**Table 9: Percentage Distribution of Area Owned by Type of Land for Each Size Class of Ownership Holding (All India) -2002-03**

| *Size Class of ownership holding (ha)* | *Under homestead* | *Agricultural land* | | | *Non-Agricultural land* | | | | *Households per size class (%)* |
|---|---|---|---|---|---|---|---|---|---|
| | | *Orchards and plantations* | *Seasonal Crop area* | *Total* | *Water bodies* | *Other non agr. Uses* | *Other* | *Total* | |
| Nil | 0 | 0 | 0 | 0 | 0 | 0 | 0 | 0 | 6.59 |
| < 0.002 | 98.84 | 0 | 0.15 | 0.15 | 0 | 0.63 | 0.39 | 1.02 | 3.44 |
| 0.002-0.005 | 99.45 | 0.02 | 1.12 | 0.14 | 0 | 0.17 | 0.24 | 0.41 | 9.65 |
| 0.005-0.040 | 93.33 | 0.12 | 4.05 | 4.17 | 0.10 | 0.76 | 1.65 | 2.51 | 20.61 |
| 0.040-0.500 | 11.59 | 2.67 | 76.68 | 79.35 | 0.55 | 0.34 | 8.17 | 9.06 | 25.97 |
| 0.500-1.000 | 4.14 | 2.51 | 83.2 | 85.71 | 0.62 | 0.42 | 9.11 | 10.15 | 13.40 |
| 1.000-2.000 | 2.50 | 2.33 | 84.68 | 87.01 | 0.45 | 0.46 | 9.59 | 10.50 | 10.82 |
| 2.000-3.000 | 1.67 | 2.13 | 84.63 | 86.76 | 0.3 | 0.48 | 10.79 | 11.57 | 4.27 |
| 3.000-4.000 | 1.17 | 3.32 | 80.03 | 83.35 | 0.36 | 0.32 | 14.8 | 15.48 | 1.75 |
| 4.000-5.000 | 0.82 | 2.17 | 84.91 | 87.08 | 0.25 | 0.37 | 11.49 | 12.11 | 1.35 |
| 5.000-7.500 | 0.93 | 2.91 | 82.22 | 85.13 | 0.38 | 0.49 | 13.09 | 13.96 | 1.18 |
| 7.500-10.00 | 0.53 | 4.56 | 73.39 | 77.95 | 0.05 | 0.53 | 20.94 | 21.52 | 0.43 |
| 10.0-20.0 | 0.60 | 1.91 | 79.27 | 81.18 | 0.24 | 0.11 | 17.87 | 18.22 | 0.46 |
| 20.0+ | 0.38 | 3.29 | 70.15 | 73.44 | 0.02 | 0.03 | 26.12 | 26.17 | 0.07 |
| All size | 3.14 | 2.58 | 81.27 | 83.85 | 0.38 | 0.39 | 12.24 | 13.01 | 100 |

*Source*: NSS Report 491

**Table 10: Percentage Distribution of Area Owned by Type of Land for Each Size Class of Ownership Holding (Orissa) – 2002-03**

| *Size Class of ownership holding (ha)* | *Under homestead* | *Agricultural land* | | | *Non-Agricultural land* | | | | *Households per size class (%)* |
|---|---|---|---|---|---|---|---|---|---|
| | | *Orchards and plantations* | *Seasonal Crop area* | *Total* | *Water bodies* | *Other non agr. Uses* | *Other* | *Total* | |
| Nil | 0 | 0 | 0 | 0 | 0 | 0 | 0 | 0 | 6.65 |
| < 0.002 | 97.13 | 0 | 0 | 0 | 0 | 0 | 2.87 | 2.87 | 3.91 |
| 0.002-0.005 | 99.52 | 0 | 0.48 | 0.48 | 0 | 0 | 0 | 0 | 10.29 |
| 0.005-0.040 | 92.09 | 0 | 6.25 | 6.25 | 0 | 0.16 | 1.5 | 1.66 | 17.55 |
| 0.040-0.500 | 9.77 | 0.18 | 87.83 | 88.01 | 0.08 | 0.14 | 1.99 | 2.21 | 34.16 |
| 0.500-1.000 | 5.76 | 0 | 90.48 | 90.48 | 0.26 | 0.06 | 3.44 | 3.76 | 14.02 |
| 1.000-2.000 | 3.97 | 0.44 | 91.63 | 92.07 | 0.48 | 0.94 | 2.54 | 3.96 | 9.73 |
| 2.000-3.000 | 2.62 | 0.02 | 92.52 | 92.54 | 0.47 | 0.07 | 4.3 | 4.84 | 2.82 |
| 3.000-4.000 | 1.74 | 8.25 | 84.64 | 92.89 | 0 | 0 | 5.38 | 5.38 | 0.90 |
| 4.000-5.000 | 1.15 | 0.02 | 92.35 | 92.37 | 0 | 0 | 6.49 | 6.49 | 0.36 |
| 5.000-7.500 | 1.5 | 1.91 | 95.46 | 97.37 | 0.03 | 0 | 1.1 | 1.13 | 0.51 |
| 7.500-10.00 | 0.12 | 0 | 99.88 | 99.88 | 0 | 0 | 0 | 0 | 0.02 |
| 10.0-20.0 | 6.63 | 5.8 | 87.2 | 93.00 | 0.13 | 0 | 0.24 | 0.37 | 0.07 |
| 20.0+ | - | - | - | - | - | - | - | - | - |
| All size | 5.58 | 0.89 | 89.92 | 90.81 | 0.27 | 0.31 | 3.03 | 3.61 | 100 |

*Source:* NSS Report No 491

**Table 11: Per 1000 Distribution of Households by Size Class of Holding of Owned Land Other than Homestead**

| *Size* | *All India* | *Orissa* |
|---|---|---|
| Nil | 416 | 385 |
| <0.002 | 2 | 1 |
| 0.002-0.005 | 2 | 1 |
| 0.005-0.040 | 18 | 14 |
| 0.040-0.50 | 234 | 328 |
| 0.50-1.00 | 132 | 137 |
| 1.00-2.00 | 106 | 92 |
| 2.00-3.00 | 38 | 24 |
| 3.00-4.00 | 18 | 10 |
| 4.00-5.00 | 12 | 3 |
| 5.00-7.50 | 11 | 5 |
| 7.50-10.0 | 4 | 0 |
| 10.0-20.0 | 5 | 0 |
| 20.0+ | 1 | 0 |

*Source*: NSS Report 491

In Orissa, on the other hand, we find 85.50% of the owner households under the marginal category, and they own 41.52% of the total area (Table 8). If we break the marginal category in size classes, as in Table 10, we find that 71.5% of the households own less than 0.5 ha each. More than half of the households in this latter size class (0-0.5 ha) own a negligible amount of productive land. Their ownership is restricted mainly to homestead land. If we exclude homestead land from our calculation, ownership landlessness increases to 38.5% from the meagre figure of 5.65% when we include homestead land. As shown in Table 11, without the homestead, the size classes above the "nil" category and up to 0.40 ha are almost emptied.

Similar is the case at the all India level. Table 9 shows that around 67 percent of households own less than 0.5 ha. Furthermore, if we exclude homestead land from our calculation (Table 11), the percentage of the landless rises to 41.6.

## The Extent of Proletarianisation

Now we come to the last part of our statistical study of the process of proletarianisation in Orissa and rural India in general. Today, even according to government data, wages have become an important source of income for farmer households, as shown by the tables 12, 13 and 14. For the landless and marginal farmer households (whose average land size is 0.40 ha.) it is the most significant source of income. At the all India level we find that for farmers in the size class <0.01, wages constitute around 78 percent of their income, and they constitute 11.62 percent of the total number of farmer households. For another 34 percent of the farmers (operating 0.01-0.40 ha of land per capita) 60 percent of their income comes from wages. But these figures include only farmer households, which are defined as households operating land. Thus, they exclude the landless (with zero operational land) whose inclusion in the data would conclusively demonstrate that in rural India a staggering majority is dependent on wage labour.

In the case of Orissa, the preponderance of wage labour is more evident. The most important source of income in the entire rural economy of the state is wages. As shown in Table 13, around 54 percent of the rural income comes from wages. The whole class of marginal farmer households, which accounts for around 82 percent of the total number in Orissa, depends mainly on wages. In fact, interestingly, possibly due to the dire state of agriculture in the region, even for a small farmer, wages constitute around 43 percent of his total income. Needless to reiterate, these figures do not speak for the totally landless wage labourers.

However, there are tremendous inter-state variations in the proportion of wage in the total income of farmer households (Table 14).

These data are definitely insufficient for explaining to us the true nature of class relations on the land, as "net receipts from cultivation" includes sharecropping income too. In recent times the nature of sharecropping arrangement has changed increasingly. The sharecroppers are being reduced, more and more, to the status of mere labourers on the land. It is the principal owner who provides capital (for buying inputs) and takes decision regarding what to produce and

**Table 12: Average Monthly Income from Different Sources, Consumption Expenditure (Rs) per Farmer Household During the Agricultural Year (July'02-June'03) (All India)**

| *Size Class* | *Wages* | *Net receipt from cultivation* | *Net receipt from farming of animals* | *Net receipt from non-farm business* | *Total income from all sources* | *Total consumption expenditure* | *wages/total income in %* | *% of total farmers* |
|---|---|---|---|---|---|---|---|---|
| <0.01 | 1075 | 11 | 64 | 230 | 1380 | 2297 | 77.90 | 11.62 |
| 0.01-0.40 | 973 | 296 | 94 | 270 | 1633 | 2390 | 59.58 | 33.96 |
| 0.41-1.00 | 720 | 784 | 112 | 193 | 1809 | 2672 | 39.80 | 27.59 |
| 1.00-2.00 | 635 | 1578 | 102 | 178 | 2493 | 3148 | 25.47 | 15.08 |
| 2.01-4.00 | 637 | 2685 | 57 | 210 | 3589 | 3685 | 17.75 | 7.86 |
| 4.01-10.00 | 486 | 4676 | 12 | 507 | 5681 | 4626 | 8.55 | 3.33 |
| >10.00 | 557 | 8321 | 113 | 676 | 9667 | 6418 | 5.76 | 0.55 |
| All sizes | 819 | 969 | 91 | 236 | 2115 | 2770 | 38.72 | 100 |

*Source*: NSS Report 497

**Table 13: Average Monthly Income from Different Sources, Consumption Expenditure and Net Investment in Productive Assets (Rs) per Farmer Household during the Agricultural Year (July'02-June'03) (Orissa)**

| *Size Class* | *Wages* | *Net receipt from cultivation* | *Net receipt from farming of animals* | *Net receipt from non-farm business* | *Total income from all sources* | *Total consumption expenditure* | *wages/total income in %* | *% of farmers households* |
|---|---|---|---|---|---|---|---|---|
| <0.01 | 578 | 0 | 17 | 71 | 666 | 2297 | 86.79 | 15.24 |
| 0.01-0.40 | 573 | 152 | 24 | 126 | 875 | 2390 | 65.48 | 33.10 |
| 0.41-1.00 | 518 | 354 | 16 | 147 | 1035 | 2672 | 50.05 | 33.29 |
| 1.00-2.00 | 613 | 705 | 23 | 84 | 1425 | 3148 | 43.02 | 13.27 |
| 2.01-4.00 | 886 | 1198 | – 46 | 418 | 2456 | 3685 | 36.07 | 4.18 |
| 4.01-10.00 | 493 | 2507 | -57 | 781 | 3724 | 4626 | 13.24 | 0.90 |
| >10.00 | 0 | 10599 | 219 | 633 | 11451 | 6418 | 0 | 0.02 |
| All sizes | 573 | 336 | 16 | 137 | 1062 | 2770 | 53.95 | 100 |

*Source*: NSS Report 497

**Table 14: Break-up of average monthly income (excl. Rent, interest, dividend etc.) per farmer household by source in each of the major States during the agricultural year 2002-03**

| State | *Average monthly income (Rs) per farmer household from* | | | | | *Wages/ Income in %* |
|---|---|---|---|---|---|---|
| | *Wages* | *Cultivation* | *Farming of animals* | *Non-farm business* | *Total* | |
| Andhra Pradesh | 643 | 743 | 93 | 155 | 1634 | 39.35 |
| Assam | 973 | 1792 | 141 | 255 | 3161 | 30.78 |
| Bihar | 497 | 846 | 265 | 202 | 1810 | 27.46 |
| Chhattisgarh | 709 | 811 | -3 | 101 | 1618 | 42.18 |
| Gujarat | 925 | 1164 | 455 | 140 | 2684 | 34.46 |
| Haryana | 1268 | 1494 | -236 | 356 | 2882 | 44.00 |
| Jammu & Kashmir | 2060 | 2426 | 382 | 620 | 5488 | 37.54 |
| Jharkhand | 924 | 852 | 86 | 207 | 2069 | 44.66 |
| Karnataka | 1051 | 1266 | 131 | 168 | 2616 | 40.17 |
| Kerala | 2013 | 1120 | 154 | 717 | 4004 | 50.27 |
| Madhya Pradesh | 560 | 996 | -227 | 101 | 1430 | 39.16 |
| Maharashtra | 799 | 1263 | 144 | 257 | 2463 | 32.44 |
| Orissa | 573 | 336 | 16 | 137 | 1062 | 53.95 |
| Punjab | 1462 | 2822 | 236 | 440 | 4960 | 29.47 |
| Rajasthan | 931 | 359 | 5 | 203 | 1498 | 62.15 |
| Tamil Nadu | 1105 | 659 | 110 | 198 | 2072 | 53.33 |
| Uttar Pradesh | 559 | 836 | 53 | 185 | 1633 | 34.23 |
| West Bengal | 887 | 737 | 77 | 378 | 2079 | 42.66 |
| All India | 819 | 969 | 91 | 236 | 2115 | 38.72 |

*Source*: NSS Report 497

how to produce. The sharecropper is a labourer who indulges in self-exploitation and whose remuneration is subject to climatic and market fluctuations. Similar is the case of "receipts from non-farm business" which may include many piece rate jobs and so on. It requires detailed micro-level researches to understand the forms of labour relations in the countryside and in the areas where rural immigrants find work.

# 3

## On the Impurity of Rural Labour

The centrality of wage-labour in defining capitalism has generally been accepted. And the above statistics show, in a definite manner, that in India (including in one of its most backward states, Orissa) too, *wage labour* has acquired a preponderant status. However, what has really confused scholars and activists is the *impure* nature of *labourers* in India. Firstly, the majority of Indians are still rural. Secondly, most of them seem to be in possession of some or other kinds of means of production – land etc, which give them a *semi-proletarian* character, instead of that of being *real proletarians*.

In mainstream sociological analyses, individuals are fitted into strict pigeonholes and then their numbers are counted to classify them. This is what can be termed as methodological individualism. Surely, in this regard, even in many advanced capitalist countries a large section of *workers* will fail the test of *purity*. Hence, proclamations like that of "the death of the working class" and the "rise of the middle class."

However, what exactly is the nature of this *impurity*? It is generally found that the income that these *individuals* draw comes, at least in part, from non-wage sources. Furthermore, we find individuals, or their families, engaged in both waged and unwaged labour. Similar issues were raised during the debate in the feminist movement in Europe and the US over housework, in the 1960s-70s. The centrality of wage labour was now understood not in terms of how many wage-labourers were to be found in society, but to what extent it re-signified all kinds of labour relations and economic activities that constitute a given socio-economic formation. Proletarianisation was understood as *a process – a process of subsumption of labour by capital*. This subsumption can be purely formal or even invisible, not actual/real or visible like wage employment of labour. In fact, the *uneven* process of labour subsumption is the basis of the labour segmentation that we find in capitalism. Massimo de Angelis points out in his recent book *The Beginning of History: Value Struggle and Global Capital*:

> ...the division between waged and unwaged activities, between public and private, between working for money and "in your own time," between production and reproduction, between work and housework, between what is valued by capital through a corresponding price tag and what is not, is the true material basis upon which the realm of the invisible that is at the basis of capital's exploitation is constructed. Because if...it is true that surplus value is the invisible value that is extracted from waged workers' labour and appropriated in the form of profit, it is also true that waged workers need to reproduce themselves, and this implies that they as well need to access the products of *others' labour*. Their dinner is prepared, their clothes washed, their health preserved thanks to invisible, objectified workers. (Emphasis original)[9]

Archaic forms of labour relations are subsumed for the benefit of capitalist accumulation. Who does not know that American slavery was the basis of the development of capitalism in the US? These forms are preserved till they become hindrances to further accumulation. The invisibility of these pre/non-capitalist forms is the basis on which visible forms are actually subsumed.

Even the *impurity* of individual labourers, whose labour process is divided between waged and unwaged phases, can be understood in this framework. As Angelis notes in the above quote, "waged workers need to reproduce themselves," and unwaged labour contributes in this reproduction. But this reproduction implies access not only to the products "others' labour," but one's own labour too. To paraphrase, she needs to prepare her dinner, her clothes have to be washed and her health preserved; this is provided for "thanks to invisible, objectified labour" – but not just others', but hers own too. This schizophrenic but real division of an individual worker is considered impurity.

Let's take a typical case. A migrant worker, who stays in a town, while his family stays back in his village, toiling on a small piece of land, is considered an *impure* worker – a semi-proletarian. Why? His *wages* are not sufficient to sustain (or *reproduce*) him or his family throughout the year, and have to be compensated by the unwaged labour of his family or his own, toiling in their own field. Hence, the function of the unwaged component of his labour (along with that of his family members) is needed to reproduce him and his family.

Under neoliberalism – an ideology of policy design that the Indian state has adopted, casualisation and contractualisation of the work process are the major methods of arranging production (and even circulation). This has led to a rapid expansion of the informal sector, which was already quite big in the pre-neoliberal phase of development in India. This assumes a vast reserve army of proletarians or surplus population, which can be "casually" used and thrown away, without many social consequences. As the data above shows, as rural India is increasingly being integrated into the neoliberal expansion of Indian capitalism, much of it is being reduced to a deposit of surplus population. The rural population in this process emerges as a vast, latent and stagnant, surplus trying to subsist (or reproduce) in the face of neoliberal land acquisition, agrarian crisis and underemployment. Subsistence agriculture in this phase is nothing but a mechanism to stabilise this surplus population, which engages in cyclical and irregular employment that the informal sector creates.

As the above analysis shows, much of the peasant

community is directly linked to capital as part-time or seasonal wage labour. Harry Cleaver says aptly in his Preface to the Mexican edition of his now classic work, *Reading Capital Politically* (1979):

> It is clear that peasants are often linked to capital quite directly through part-time waged labour. This is the only role usually recognized...as a "working class function." The problem with the usual analysis is partly methodological. There is an attempt to classify people into one category or another by their dominant role. If a worker works most of the year in a factory then that worker is classified as a member of the working class. If a person lives on the land most of the time, then that person is a peasant, not a worker. This is stupid. What we should see is that there are many roles or functions played by the working class in its relation to capital, and that *individuals move from one function to another at different points in time*. When a worker is in the factory, that worker is a productive worker. When that same worker is at home doing housework or working on the land in subsistence agriculture, the function has changed - now we are in the sphere of the reproduction of labour power – but the worker is still a worker, still part of the working class.
>
> When a peasant takes a few days or weeks to look for waged work, that peasant passes from the latent to the floating reserve army. *If there are no jobs, after a while the worker will pass back from the floating to the latent role.* If there is a job, then for a while the worker will be part of the waged labour force instead of being unwaged. *There is no change in class status here, only a change in the form of the relationship with capital!* All persons who are forced to work for capital – either reproducing themselves as labour power in the latent or floating reserve army or actually producing a product – are part of that working class. The form of the imposition of work is secondary.
>
> *But what, some may ask, of the peasants who produce a surplus they sell on the market? Are these not petty bourgeois producers and outside the working class?* The answer is that *they are still very much part of the working class if the result of their work is only self-reproduction*. (Emphasis added)[10]

# 4

# Political Implications

## Identity and Class

If disparity among geographical locations or sectors or communities is the ground for rural mobilisation and struggle, then the political strategy that evolves will not be geared towards structural transformation, but towards creating parity. It will be restricted to fighting for social inclusion. Such struggles will tend to hide internal differentiation, and will depoliticise local conflicts, while stressing on homogeneity at the identitarian level – on the basis of locations, community or sector etc. On the other hand, the centrality of labour and class struggle allows us to radicalise popular mobilisation and struggle by making every conflict and contradiction into a node for politics. Classes are not internally homogeneous – however, class struggle unlike identity struggle does not require homogeneity. Even labour market segmentation can be a ground for class struggle, by which the internalised hegemony is questioned – a struggle against the whiteness of the white worker, waged by the black working class, is a fight for working class unity and against the internalisation of hegemonic structures by the working class. This perspective on class struggle gives us the opportunity to understand and engage with identitarian movements too.

Ambedkar's understanding of the caste system is very relevant in this regard. He did not consider the struggle against caste a struggle for identity assertion, or for mutual toleration among diverse communities. It was not a struggle for mere representation. He called for the "annihilation of caste." In fact, Ambedkar had a subtle conception of caste, which could help us transcend the dichotomy of caste and class. During his days in his Independent Labour Party (ILP) and in his piece "Who were the Shudras?" (1946), Ambedkar viewed caste not as a purely cultural edifice, but as the carrier of specific work functions. The caste system transformed "the scheme of division of work into a scheme of division of workers, into fixed and permanent occupational categories." So the annihilation of the caste system will pave the way for the transcendence of the material and ideological division of workers. But it is important to reassert that the class or the "labour" perspective cannot remain blind to the internal configuration of the class. Class unity is posed not by wishing away the internal divisions within the working class; rather it is a product of class struggle, of struggle against the foundation of those divisions – of intra-class competition and hierarchisation.

## The Land Question

As our statistical analysis, coupled with the conceptual issues that we discussed above, indicates, the majority of rural Indians are today proletarianised, in the sense that they toil for self-reproduction, alternating between wage employment and subsistence self-employment. This fact can give a new insight into the nature of rural struggles today. It is definitely true that the National Rural Employment Guarantee Act (NREGA) that the Indian state has provided to the rural poor gives them a tremendous opportunity to come out of their invisibility. By a single act of legislation, a vast rural labour market has become visible, with millions constituting a surplus population which is emerging out of its latency. But the partial guarantee that this bestows on the rural poor has only marginally altered their invisible status – as the hidden underemployed, and the footloose labour alternating between wage employment and subsistence self-employment.

Another important implication of the above analysis is that it redefines the whole land question. The land issue has generally been associated with *the peasant question – peasant hunger for land*. But now, with the emergence of a new perspective, the land issue is increasingly been posed as a *question of labour*, associated with *workers' need to self-reproduce*. A poor tribal who tills a small plot illegally in the forest area is doing so not to satisfy his hunger for land, but in order to survive.

Earlier the land question was posed as an issue which relates to the development of agriculture – would land redistribution increase productivity or would concentration work better?

> ...the many popular struggles over land today are driven by experiences of the fragmentation of labour (including losses of relatively stable wage employment in manufacturing and mining, as well as agriculture), by contestations of class inequality, and by collective demands and actions for better conditions of living ('survival', stability of livelihood, economic security), and of which the most dramatic instances are land invasions and occupations. There is now a revival and restatement of the significance of struggles over land to the social dynamics and class politics of the 'South' during the current period of globalization and neo-liberalism... Contemporary land struggles are significantly different from the ('classic') peasant movements of the past, and are much more rooted in the semi-proletarian condition: that of *'a workforce in motion, within rural areas, across the rural-urban divide, and beyond international boundaries'*.[11]

This is not to say that land is now *exclusively* a labour question. Far from it. The dominant discourse in movements against land acquisition, like the POSCO struggle in Orissa, still poses it as an issue of "agriculture" versus "industry", "rural" versus "urban". The only submission that we make here is that regions like coastal Orissa have high rural differentiation, and the homogeneity that we witness today might be temporary and even deceptive. Within these land movements, a working class viewpoint is emerging towards land and development in general, which is not vocalised by the leadership.

# Notes

1. David Harvey (2005) *Spaces of Neoliberalization: Towards a Theory of Uneven Geographical Development*, Franz Steiner Verlag, p. 60.
2. David Harvey (1982) *Limits to Capital*, Verso, p. 417.
3. Rajni Kothari (1970) *Politics in India*. Originally published by Little Brown and Company, reprinted in *The Writings of Rajni Kothari*, Orient BlackSwan, 2009, p. 124.
4. "Presidential Address at All India Kisan Conference (9 April 1939)", *Selected Works of Acharya Narendra Deva Volume 1*, Nehru Memorial Museum & Library (1998)
5. Quoted in Arvind N. Das (1982) "Peasants and Peasant Organisations: The Kisan Sabha in Bihar", *Journal of Peasant Studies*, 9(3):40-87
6. V I Lenin, "Capitalism in Agriculture", in Utsa Patnaik (2007), *The Agrarian Question in Marx and his Successors Volume 1*, LeftWord, p. 299.
7. Vijay Paul Sharma (2007) "India's Agrarian Crisis and Smallholder Producers' Participation in New Farm Supply Chain Initiatives: A Case Study of Contract Farming", IIM Ahmedabad.
8. C P Chandrashekhar and Jayati Ghosh (2004) "The Possibilities of Land Reform", MacroScan.
9. Massimo de Angelis (2007) *The Beginning of History: Value Struggle and Global Capital*, Pluto, p. 57.
10. Harry Cleaver, *Una Lectura Politica de El Capital*, México: Fondo de Cultura Económica, 1985.
11. Henry Bernstein (2004) "Changing Before Our Very Eyes': Agrarian Questions and the Politics of Land in Capitalism Today', *Journal of Agrarian Change*, Vol. 4 Nos. 1 & 2.